Someday the Plan of a Town

Someday the Plan of a Town

poems

TODD BOSS

W. W. NORTON & COMPANY
Independent Publishers Since 1923

For information about permission to reproduce selections from this book,
write to Permissions, W. W. Norton & Company, Inc.,
500 Fifth Avenue, New York, NY 10110

For information about special discounts for bulk purchases, please contact
W. W. Norton Special Sales at specialsales@wwnorton.com or 800-233-4830

Map illustrations © Pamela Gerbrandt. Used by permission.

Book design by Chris Welch
Manufacturing by Versa Press
Production manager: Lauren Abbate

ISBN 978-0-393-88140-0

W. W. Norton & Company, Inc., 500 Fifth Avenue, New York, N.Y. 10110
www.wwnorton.com

W. W. Norton & Company Ltd., 15 Carlisle Street, London W1D 3BS

1 2 3 4 5 6 7 8 9 0

for Mallory

CONTENTS

AN APPROACH TO THIS BOOK

In June 2018, I sold nearly everything I owned, gave up my Minneapolis apartment (only half-facetiously writing "Trump" on the "Reason for leaving" line of the Lease Cancellation form) and began house-sitting my way around the world.

I suspected it would get old fast. I figured I might go six months or so before growing exhausted by nonstop travel, and return to my things, my friends, my family. Instead, I circled the globe for the next two years as a solo traveler, rarely requiring hotel accommodations, stringing thirty consecutive house-sitting gigs together using TrustedHousesitters.com—and it was nothing short of invigorating.

You might say I was already primed for such a journey. I was still reeling from losing the things that mattered most to me: My twenty-year marriage had ended in acrimony, my daughter and I were estranged, my son was in full rebellion mode, my creative projects seemed fruitless, and my country was in the throes of a slobbering authoritarian delirium. Somehow despite my grief and confusion, I convinced myself I deserved a one-way ticket out.

I found myself alternately inhabiting thatched-roof farmhouses, hillside estates, urban apartments, and lush gardens in Berlin, Barcelona, Marrakesh, Singapore, Auckland. House-sitting gigs often came complete with pets or livestock for which I was responsible. I tended sheep from a stone cabin in the Pyrénées. I minded two sleepy cats in a Tuscan villa, a coop full of unruly chickens in London, and a playful puppy on the Gold Coast of Australia.

Whereas once my creative practice had me "working from home," now I worked from strangers' homes. I was house-sitting for free—no cash changed hands—but it meant that my only living expenses were travel and food. Sometimes I rented a car, sometimes the owners let me use theirs, but more often it was mass transit that got me where I needed to go: the streetcar line was just outside my apartment in Vienna, the downtown river ferry stopped three blocks from my house in Brisbane. I didn't trouble myself to "see the sights." I wanted, instead, to live like a local, soak up the vibes, learn the streets. I walked and walked and walked.

When you're unburdened by material concerns, it's much easier to be present to the world around you. This is why travel enchants—not because every place is more attractive than the place you've left behind, but because you've left behind more than a place. You've left behind the burdens and clutter, the stack of bills waiting to be paid. On the road to this day, I have no lawn to mow, no roof to patch, no driveway to shovel, no storage to manage. I have only two carry-on suitcases to my name. I am living the extraordinary luxury of less.

On hearing about my travels, people often ask me to name my favorite homestay or my favorite city. I tell them it's impossible. I fell in love with *every single one*. This makes for a lousy shorthand, but I can't possibly detail two years of enchantment. I want to tell them, for example, about the little crossroads town in the Charente where the quiet black creek ran beneath a mill ruin, just as equally as I want to tell them about the poolside hacienda in the Yucatán where the neighborhood's open-air bars filled up at night with hardworking people, smoking and drinking in the doorways, their faces roseate against street-lit pastels. I really did: I fell in love everywhere I went. If I wasn't enchanted on arrival, inevitably I was enchanted by the time I left, by the animals in my charge, of course, but also by the particular quirks, colors, and rhythms of my adopted homes and haunts.

The poems in this book are my only souvenirs. Most of them were written at strangers' kitchen tables, across irregular time zones, in countries where English is seldom spoken, far from everything I'd once taken for granted. They were written under the influence of long walks along the Thames, the South Sea, the Pacific. Their opening lines occurred to me at farmer's markets, strudel bars, train stations, and mountaintop basilicas. To my mind, they still taste of chili peppers, smell of cedar, or whisper of tavern music. And yet, they concern the most domestic of matters.

I returned to the United States just as the pandemic's border-closings rendered passports virtually worthless. The world was being invited, at tremendous cost, to re-evaluate its patterns and its privileges. A burning curtain revealed how very fragile our interdependent systems really are.

An epic global migration, caused largely by climate change but exacerbated by fear-driven socioeconomic policymaking, will characterize the coming century. We are soon to become a planet of nomads, trading the known for the unknown, increasingly dependent upon one another, forced to content ourselves with less.

Let go. Pack light. Take care of one another.

Todd Boss

Someday the Plan of a Town

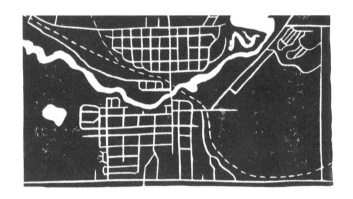

Where You've Been

The trouble with telling people
where you've been

is that then they start telling you
where they've been

and making it sound like
you haven't been

anywhere till you've been
where they've been,

and before you can tell them
that where you've been

is every bit as interesting as
where they've been,

they're explaining how to get
to where they've been

even though you don't intend
to go—and by then

where you've been's been
lost around the bend,

and you know they know,
though nobody says so,

that no one's going
to be going there again.

Vienna, Austria

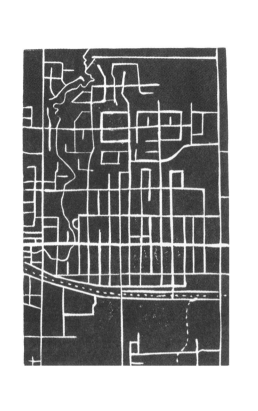

Someday the Plan of a Town

—right down to its sidetracks and back
alleyways—will match—or so goes
the dream—with some identical patch
of neural network your rogue thoughts
roam in—overlay it like those musculo-
skeletal transparencies with which
anatomy textbooks come bound—and
you'll be at home in its dogleg jointwork
of cobbled kinks—and your body will
resound at every fork, tuning-fork–like—
and every road you ever rambled will be
re-scrambled to appear to have brought
you here, where you fit so perfectly, where
you can practically predict where to find
every bench or postbox, and where you
can cue every little old lady who leaves
her flat to buy bread—as if she were
locking up a little room in your head
and trading your idea of money for your
idea of food before returning to wipe
her shoes on the mat your mind's laid flat
and fit her flat key to its shoulder into
the strike plate keyhole through which you
daily romance her as she grows older—
that worn, dome-topped slot that looks
as if two question marks met on the road
to kiss and mate and make one question
opening, opening—each forever the
other's only answer.

Tarifa, Andalucía, Spain

He Divides His Time Between

is a line I
always wanted
in my bio.

"He divides his
time between
Reykjavík and
Sandusky, Ohio."

"He summers
on Lake Como
and winters
in Aspen."

As it happens,
noplace *is*
like home.

Already I split
my attentions
between
this world
and any halfway
decent poem.

Doctors
call it deficit,
but some
divisions make
surpluses.

We multiply
when we divide
our lives, our

loves, and our
addresses.

Last year, I kept
40+ pets (house-
sitting for
strangers is as
varied as it
gets) dividing
12 months
into 20 sits in
16 countries on
5 continents.

I had a married
life before, in a
subdivision of
peace and war.

In equal thirds
my loved ones
ate my heart
like a festival
roast.

Now my father's
son is a ghost,
a wisp of smoke,
a metaphor.

He divides his
time between
nothing and
much and
matters and
anymore.

Greenville, South Carolina, USA

In Elaborate Museums

on cul-de-sacs: curators

of artifacts. Keepers of
grounds and statuary.

Security constabulary.
Feather-dusting figurines.

Cars, boats, trampolines.
Temperature-controlled

garages. Boudoirs fit
for maharajas. Snap-top

plastic storage tubs
stacked in rented storage

hubs—albatrosses ill-
afforded, hoarded, sorted,

and exported from their
owners' mini-mansions,

waiting for their
wing expansions.

Austin, Texas, USA

Essentials

I'm down to two bags.
I use a friend's address.

I've only got one last
recurring nightmare

that forces me to face
my ex. There's still one

child I haven't lost, but
he's next. Even our loved

ones are non-essential,
sorry to report. You've

come here for news of
how to live, but grieve

and grieve is all I can say.
Grieve enough, you

can even get grieving
out of the way. Grief's

chiefest among chores.
Do it well, and the mostly

empty universe is
yours.

Page, Arizona, USA

Golds Within

Like the tavern owner
negotiating with
the contractor over
the entryway color,
like the corner grocer
sorting the order
in the morning before
opening, we artists
are keeping going
our poor concerns.
Last night while I
meant to be sleeping,
I was bent over one
unkempt square meter,
fussing for more
than an hour. The night
before, I went up a
metaphorical ladder
and found so much
to do up there it was
dawn by the time
I came down. Is it
worth it, or is it a
quackery, to work so
exquisite a taquerie
or so outré an atelier
so far from the heart
of town—to lavish
our grief and our
glee in them, to
belabor a life in the
feeble belief that
someone might see
what we see in them?

A job at Daimler-Benz
building cars, the
whistle blowing us
into the bars—ours
aren't assembly line
aspirations, we're
driven to something
worse. No pension
awaits. Art's never
done doing. There's
always another machine
wants unscrewing,
always a richer beer
that needs brewing,
and this is our cure
and our curse. Our
beautiful things fill
the halls of kings, we
ought to have it made.
But the straw we spin
spins golds within,
an undervalued braid.

Vienna, Austria

The Wobbling, Body-Long Bubble of Concern

was brought down around you
by the cosmic bubble blower before
you were born, an uber-womb
you'll be born from only when
you die. You wear it everywhere,

and when your self-concern
turns from your own to someone
else's troubles, then your and
the other person's bubbles merge
into a newer, bigger bubble with a

wider wobble, no matter how far
from one another you go. One can
consider (easily so) that the world
is little more than a bubbulous
agglimmeration of polymorphous

Venns—Venns whose intersections
contain and recontain. On a plane,
my concern fills the cabin. In an Uber
or a bus, my concern encompasses
both or all of us. If a fellow citizen

doubts aloud my patriotism, I can
feel the wobble in my bosom, but I
cannot exclude him. And when I'm
gone and my bubble is burst, it won't
be lost on those who were in it, whether

they knew they were in it or not, not
for a minute. For I believe (again, so

easily) that love is more a practice
than a test, and that it is felt or lends a
shimmer or offers comfort no matter

if it's unexpressed, and well after it's
given, and that its sudden shatter
is soundless and invisibly beautiful,
like the drying of a kiss is, a shape
unshaping itself into a billion blisses.

Washington, DC, USA

The One About the Taxi

is famous
around here

but nobody
tells it

anymore. You
can live here

for years, as
I have, and

catch it only
once, standing

at the bar or
wherever.

What is it
about those

funny little
lies? You can

never get one
when you

want one
and then you

get one and
it's a surprise.

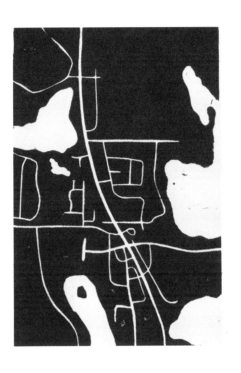

The Mind Will Wander

—as water will seep;
as mice will yonder

creep the clover deep
and still nose home;

as a wren will dither
daily in the dome and

remember the nest's
address; as honeybees

comb September after
nectar—so the mind

will wander between
the lines (of music or

news or conversation),
will spend attention on

wonder's fine wines,
will even tend toward

understanding, and,
laden with whimsy's

flimsy pollens, survive
to wend a way back

to the studious hive
and the subject at hand.

Everything I Have Has Humps and Hooves

—everything rouses and grunts and moves
with stiff resolve from day to day (my loves,
my dreams, my appetites). Away, along the grooves
of dunes, my mornings and my afternoons,
away they rock on creaking clogs of bone
(my prayers, my doubts, my fears of being left alone)
built to endure, and long.
                              And still, too soon
I know each one will grind the pestles of its knees
into the sand, not far from some mirage of trees,
where I will find it sagging broken where it lies
in a cloud of flies.
                              Everything I have will stray,
my bundled caravans unstrung and swept away.
And if I try to call them back (my joys, my shames)
I'll find I can't recall their names.

I Know You Feel You're the Wyeth Girl and that the Farmhouse Yonder

is *the comfort of being loved* whereas
the broad sloping field of rye beneath
that stubborn sky of sheeted steel stands
for *the mortifying ordeal of being known*
and I know how you're painted so I can
appreciate this gloss on the composition
and your distress the girl turned away in
a canted position in her cotton dress a
representation I guess of yearning and yet

I say look still somehow it's a beautiful
day despite the palette of mid-tone gray
in fact rarely in art is seen a field so green
and that surely as you cross between the
lower left corner of your heart's expanse
and the settled upper right surely there might
come that unexpected break of raking light
that any hopeful soul will recognize and
also likely butterflies.

after a meme based on Andrew Wyeth's painting
"Christina's World"

Workmen Discarding a Parquet Floor, Vienna

Into the dumpster goes
someone's square
                    feet.
The racket royally
        rattles
the street. It's a four-
handed
        band performing
the complete
works of Beethoven
    using only
wooden castanets
                    in
incomplete sets. What
    once a woman
        danced
across. What
    once in a sash
                    of sun
the cat snoozed
afternoons
        upon.
    Un-glued, un-
patterned, going,
gone. But first this
                    tuneless
rhythm-less out-
                    pouring
of flooring into
        the bin.
Where once
            a couple,
just moved in, lay
    in sin.

Where once first
          steps a
toddler took. And
            fell.
Maybe a spill made it
swell
and split. Maybe the
            new
owners just don't
fancy it.
            Well,
it's dated, no doubt.
So last century or
        the century
         before.
It's out.
           Cue
the two-man crew
         who,
bent with bar of crow
and barrowed
         wheel,
         go
wall to wall to haul it all
  away. The next act
in this play
may play on other
        boards,
but it better be better
  than whatever
went before,
        because
loud and long is
      the floor's
      applause.

Encore, encore,
      it calls.

Why Empty Barber Shops Draw Me, I Don't Know

—it's romantic. I
end up snapping

photos through the
windows: chair

convened there by
chair, by chair,

mirrored, clean,
someone the night

before having
swept up all the

cut hair, light
streaming in from

the street printing
whatever's on the

plate glass crooked
across the floor,

CLOSED sign askew
in the door. We do

want community,
we do—but we also

don't, we want to be
held close & left

alone, we want
to talk when we want

to talk & we want
sometimes instead

to sit quietly while
someone touches us

all about the head
with the edges of a

scissoring scissor
& the neat teeth

of a comb. Small
comfort, but lucky

for us, the wealthy
as well as the poor,

that there are
a few things left

in this old world
we still need other

people for.

Baltimore, Maryland, USA

When the Sommelier Farts

he lifts his nose and blurts:
"I'm getting dried berry . . .
flint . . . mocha notes . . .
hints of honeydew melon,
and oak . . ."
     and it's no joke;
he actually is.
      Our arts
are louder than our hearts—
we wear them like
iconoclasts wear clothes.

The florist's may be rose,
but the same world passes
through the sommelier's
rosé-colored glasses. Your
basic mud and grasses
are, in the right snuffle,
truffle. Some people
don't see people, only
people-shaped graces.
How they do it
      Heaven
knows. Some arts are bigger,
bolder, more fruit-forward
than others, that's just
how it goes. *De gustibus*
non est disputandum,

which is to say:
                When
farts the sommelier,
it's just another big bouquet.

And who would have it
any other way?

        Fish Creek, Wisconsin, USA

The Keenest Blade

would—wouldn't it—end
in a cutting edge an

atom thin? And in
fact one such has been,

by folks who find things,
found—obsidian

among ruins.
A blade of stone

with an edge so fine
it doesn't cut, exactly,

         but

divides
      among
           things,

sorting
with every stroke.

Translucent if you
hold it to the light,

too fragile to be used,
and made, they think,

for making's sake,
for pride. *You can*

hone a blade till there
is no blade,

Franz Wright rightly
wrote. And if it's true

we murder to dissect,
what crime's mere

differentiating do?
Even blunt things

wedge the world apart.
But all is one.

Distinction fades.
I'm done

with sharpening and
sharpening blades.

Minneapolis, Minnesota, USA

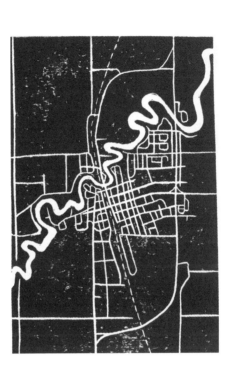

Be Glad Your Parents Fucked

you up. What luck you're
far from flawless, right?
Well-adjusted people
frighten most folk, or get
stuck in well-adjusted
paper-pushers' jobs. Be
glad it was half-assed,
the job your parents did
on you. You'd rather be
whole-assed—or worse,
no-assed-at-all?
　　　　　Artists in
Japan hex off perfection,
marring prints that lift
too clean off inky blocks
of wood. The perfect *is*
the enemy of the good.
Be glad your parents hid
your fineness underneath
a well-placed scar. How
awful people would be
to you if they knew how
faultless you actually are.

after Philip Larkin
San Francisco, California, USA

At the Sofitel

in Budapest, alone,
regretting leaving,
      estranged from
      my daughter six
      years almost,
            believing it might
            be six and six more
            before she texts or
                  answers when I call,
                  trying to remember
                  how it all began,
                        I find that I can.
                        Every ball thrown
                        at her, every tear,
                              every tatter. Very
                              matter-of-factly now
                              I can recall exactly.

Even so, I saw her
at the funicular
today, in her
      old winter downs,
      12 years younger,
      chattering away!
            I reached to help
            her up before
            I became aware
                  she had her own
                  father there,
                  clutching his pass.
                        And we rose
                        while I fell,
                        the tall Sofitel

and the Danube
gliding away
outside the glass.

Sophie, tell your
story. Say you're
sorry or not sorry.
    Sophie, tell of
    life, your studies,
    your plans. From
        Sofitel to Sofitel
        I go, it's a mockery,
        soundproof doors
            closing behind me
            as if a quiet so bad
            could be improved.
                Sophie. Tell Dad
                how much longer
                you plan to be
                    the stronger one, un-
                    moving, unmovable,
                    unmoved.

Budapest, Hungary

A Shrug of Boys

in twos and threes
is mostly shoes. The
one in front's got
least to lose, while
those in back wear
last year's kicks.
One's come undone,
and doesn't care.
And that one there's
outgrown his pair,
they pinch, it cramps
his gait. But wait—
they re-configurate.
It's hard to tell now
which one calls the
play. It seems a
team decision's
underway—but I'm
no fool. They do not
teach you this in
school but privilege
does what privilege
is. Only one gets
picks. The mall is
his.

Seville, Spain

The Sculptor Made a Giant of the Boy

1.

The sculptor
made a giant of the boy
who killed the giant
with his slingshot
big as a hammock
and his rock

as big as a boy.
He made his brow
Neanderthal,
triangulating for
the viewer's
gaze, so he's

not to size
in more ways
than immediately
meets the eyes.
Chiseled
and chiseled

from a 12-ton stone
in the heart of town
lying down,
one historian
describes him rising
from the marble math

"like a person being
slowly revealed as
water drains
from a bath."

Machines to hoist
and move the kid

had yet to be
invented, so they did
a ropy frame on
a greasy skid
till—bare,
twisted on one

dropped hip,
balanced on one
foot, supported
by the other lifted—
there he stood
in the square—

a marble
elegance, a
paragon of power,
naiveté in its
finest hour,
bold

gaze fixed
on a distance
that—
in a minute—
would have a
giant in it,

stone cold,
laid out flat.

*My mind could not stop imagining it. An earthquake hits the center of
Florence. Liquid waves roll under the rigid city: The church bells ring
out of time, terra cotta tiles rain down from the Renaissance rooftops,*

priceless paintings rattle off the walls of the Uffizi. Meanwhile, inside the Accademia Gallery, the David's pedestal begins to tilt. Slightly at first, just enough to shift the statue's gaze. so that he looks not at his old enemy anymore----the implied Goliath off in the distance----but at a new one: the floor he's been standing on for 134 years. . . .

Finally, the compromised ankles reach their angle of maximum stress. They begin to slide along the old microfracture faults----an earthquake within the earthquake----and the David's legs and ankles are crushed by the weight of the body above. He begins to truly fall.

The first thing to hit the floor is his left elbow, the arm that holds the heroic sling. and it bursts . . . Then the rest of the marble will meet the floor, and the physics from there will be fast and simple: force, resistance, the brittleness of calcite crystals, the shearing of microscopic grains along the axes on which they align. Michelangelo's David will explode.

----*Sam Anderson in* The New York Times

2.

Denying the boy
a shock-proof
plinth, Italy
takes a terrible
chance: Each
thunder or
underground
rumble makes

David's varicose
fissures
advance. Little
by little he
heads for a
stumble, our
soldier sans pants,
our humble young

prankster. We
couldn't or wouldn't or
didn't do a thing,
and the stone
has long since left
the sling

so the cracks
up the backs
of his ankles
floss
transvisible as
arachnid's goss,
a crumble
marbling
the marvelous
marble that
dates to its
quarry in
Carrara's moss.

And when,
nose to nose
with that last
disaster at
last he goes,
he'll be blasted
into scattershot as
brittle-white as bone

—just like that
which
flaked
around him
when at first
the master
found him
in the stone.

In the room the women come and go
Talking of Michelangelo.

—T. S. Eliot, "The Love Song of J. Alfred Prufrock"

Granite contains much oxygen and is relatively light. It "floats." When
granite forms under the earth's crust, great chunks of it bob up, I read
somewhere, like dumplings.

—Annie Dillard, Teaching a Stone to Talk

3.

And then we'll live
in a post-David world
—like the pre-David
world but aware
he once existed—
although, pre-Michel-
angelo, they knew
of David from the Bible,
so . . .

Of flesh made word
and flesh made stone,
immortality favors
one. Words
set man in stone
more so than stone,
but even they, someday,
like granite in reverse,
beneath earth's surface
will submerse at last
when all is done,
and with our stories
of the universe gone,
our sun will be nothing

but a sun, our moon
a moon
like every other one.

And there'll be
no such thing as man.
And there'll be
no such thing as art.
And there'll be
anymore such things
as boys or wars
or stones or slings.
The world
will fly apart.

And God,
if there should be a God,
will go at last alone,
unsung, unwritten,
and unseen,
the bash
from smash to finish
past,

the slate of Him again

wiped clean.

Parenting You

is th e bull.   And m   e,

at be st I'm   rider, clamping
          h   is hat.
    It's a   ll   I can do,
      sta   ying on to p o f

Parenting You. I   m   ostl y
        f la il.   I t   ry
            to s   t ay
    th is way o   f   t   ail.

          De   rv ish   !
          Such b ent
s   port, th e man m   is-

    fixed up   on t   h e b r ute
    until he 's n   ot: a kno t of

            dir t.
    It   p lays like w   ork, th en
          s   wer   ves like
          s wing. O   nly

al   ways dis   or i   en ting . And

    y   o   u   ,

    yo u'   r e c lou   d, y   ou' re
      r   in g, yo u' re crow   d ,
    yo   u're sting.

Y   ou   'r e

rope.   Y ou're ho   pe   .

Y   ou're e ve ry   t h in   g .

Page, Arizona, USA

Runaway Bus

For a while—maybe a mile or more—a boy no
more than four overhangs my seat so he can see
my fingers on the keys of my laptop power away
as we motor Hwy 4 through Runaway Bay

+ for that mile, I write for his amusement alone,
highlighting a word + randomly replacing it,
lumping whole lines + bumping them up + down
the poem's column, tracing + retracing a FIND

+ REPLACE that turns all the *and*s into plus signs
+ back again, riding my most reckless impulses
like a surfer crushing madly into the barrel of
a wave, knowing that if I don't hit SAVE, I can

UNDO the vandalism done, but then the kid + his
dad get off the bus + my fun goes with them +
so does my rhythm. So I put the verse in reverse
+ watch as every stop flies past again, fast

+ faster, a bus barreling backward along its own
Coastal Hwy, toward its own original disaster
+ it all seems so unreal, my only passenger
gone, that I let go the wheel + let it all be undone,

the roadway a rip curl of words going under
till the run disappears + the sheet goes foam-
white + I spill out onto the street + walk home,
unwilling to write anymore tonight,

my mojo spent, the ocean still swelling, its epic
grandly un-telling itself into the sand . . . + I sleep
like a man comfortably dead, route driven +
heart read.

Runaway Bay, Queensland, Australia

Nine Voices at St. Martin's

I am not a believer, nor
do I believe
in disbelief. I'm not too
proud for anything,
and neither facts
nor fictions frighten me.
I'm comfortable
holding a stranger's gaze,
and I often feel god or
something godly
gazing back. My life is
full of the usual
urgent necessary and
unnecessary distractions,
but yesterday,
in London with a friend,
I descended into the
crypt café and then
wandered upward into St.
Martin's where a choir
of nine was not so much
singing as releasing birds
of hymnody into the airy
sanctuary, lilting flocks
of wingy sounds, and
by the time they finally
began "Abide with Me,"
I was openly weeping
in my row, my friend
kindly nesting my hand,
and the world took on
that forest glade glow
it gets when you know
beauty may be found,

and suddenly this simple,
sturdy, clear-windowed
temple with its weather-
vane steeple was my
favorite of all Europe's
showy churches, and
London's people seemed
the finest people, and it
didn't seem at all odd
to find myself here, that
there should be a god,
or that God, whether
soul or energy or light,
might be right there,
abiding in the patterns of
voices in mid-flight, or
the patter of rain on
Duncannon Street.
I mopped my face
with my pocket square and
stuffed it back away
and wanted more, would've
stayed all day, but
one more tune and they
were done, and filed away
behind the altar,
where, no doubt they
folded their books and packed
their packs and bloomed
their umbrellas into
the afternoon and crossed
into the underground and
queued ordinarily
for the train. If I passed
one going home, I didn't
recognize, I didn't know
to praise them

for my opened ears,
my opened eyes,
the music my own train
made as it wheeled,
the colors of the sky,
 the brick towns passing by,
the trees on the ridgeline,
and the horses in the field.

London, England

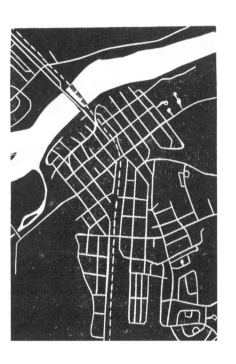

Fairer

The claw marks in my neck
long faded, the steam of hate
evaporated, attempted identity theft
subverted, assets, passwords, passport
converted, accusations of assault
reversed, two years' court fees
reimbursed, restraining orders at last
elapsed, libelous campaigns
collapsed, attempts to turn my friendships
rotten and threats of murder and vengeance
forgotten, I'm
finally ready
—whatever comes next—
to re-engage
the fairer sex.

If You're Not Doing Her Sheets

you're not doing her
right. If you want her
to find you delicious,
do her

dishes and she might.
This one goes hot
as an oven
for a man in an

apron. For this one
nothing's sexier
than when a
man handles her

vacuum cleaner.
The leaner meats
can't compete
with the fatter if,

once the latter's
wiener feast is
over, he's
wiping down

the splatter. A
little soap
and hot water
and a girl's

in a lather.
Forget your
barroom blather,
she'd rather

you blow her
mind by coming
home at 5 and
blowing her

drive and the
spot where she
parks. A pilot
might light sparks

but it's the steward
who apprehends her
needs just by
meeting her gaze

who fans the blaze.

Lourmarin, Vaucluse, France

Temp

Said I'd
tie her
to the
radiator
later
made her
temp
go up a
touch her
next text
revealed
as much
& then?
it got
my water
heater
humming
then we
bang I'm
thumbing
till we're
dripping
hot &
now it's
porn I'm
ripping
silks &
shucking
shorts &
dropping
to the
worn
hard
wood

floor
buttons
skipping
like
popping
field
fucking
corn.

San Francisco,
California. USA

A Man Pulls a Sweater Over His Shirt

First, he's got to un-invert inside-
out parts outside-right, and, wrangling
the whole thing roughly into a loop, rope
himself about the neck, and, with a flick,
free up the mane at the back. Next
comes that mummery of wrists by
which, in summary, fists clamp stiffly
over shirtsleeve ends to keep them from
disappearing during the endearing
rearranging of limb and clothing that's
coming. Now then. Up into his own
cable knits he dives, both fistfuls at
once, in order to work, with a plumping
motion, the scarf-like commotion of
cotton more open. He's a god of muffled
thunder shoulder high in a churning
cloud formation. At last, one arm at a
time must find and climb into its funnel,
elbows winching by twists. The empty
lists of tunnel fill up with checks as
sleeve with sleeve is matched. Each
diver survives, emerges, its clutch of
cuff intact, released. As if handling
something hot from the oven, he shakes
the whole chore off, then slices a
scissors of fingers back into each bunchy
nozzle to puzzle his unbuttoned barrel
flaps flat on skin over catch of watch or
kink of bracelet latch. It seems he's won
the match—but wait, he isn't done. One
thumb goes thumbs-down into the collar
where its job is to fix what's riding there
and confirm the tag's not flagging, while
his other hand is nagging his Oxford's

box plate straight, re-stuffing it into the
band of his pant so the rumpled jumper
can fall flatter. (And sir, while you're
down there: a pinky, discreetly slipped,
can doublecheck that things are zipped.)
Then it's only a scant matter of luffing
the pullover's lower quarter to be certain
it isn't caught, and that it curtains where
it ought. And now, the horse's blanket
straight, he's ready for the saddle, pack,
or whatever weights await at work, at the
service of city slicker or farmer.
Thicker. And a little warmer.

Vienna, Austria

Men, Then, Maybe

How to say it not louche:
Men too've got lashes as
lovely sometimes, their
locks sometimes as lush.
Couldn't I love one just as
much, and touch one just
as generously? Men are as
leisurely over the Sunday
paper Sunday mornings,
aren't they? Linger over
coffee just as languorously
don't they? I'll admit,
my gaze is lately on them
more than formerly a bit.
Here I get to harmlessly
wondering how seamlessly
this one's arm heavily
linked on mine might be.
Or how might that one's
shapely upper lip between
my top and bottom fit.
Men aren't faultless, oh, I
know. Now and then a prick,
okay, but let's just say the
"fairer" blooms I've picked
so far, though lovely, are
no prick-less clutch. So,
men, then. Maybe. Huh.
The hot mechanics may yet
be a mystery, but at least
I know the parts already.
A body's a body, after all,
a tenderness a tenderness.
Probably we'd most of us

be better off genderless.
A martyred saint for the
desert storms of your
hetero-norms anymore,
I ain't. Sorry. So, strip me
of my rank, and shave me.
Issue the smart khaki
shirt and tent. Save me
a spot near the flag up
front. Gimme a nickname.
Start me a grunt.

Auckland, New Zealand

My Book Open on Top of His

face down on a leather
        couch—splayed—spines
aligned—two bodies of work
    one body—my poetry—
        his prose—
or are they birds—mating
mid-glide where there are
        no words—no cover—
one featherweight lover
    on another feather-
    weight lover—so—
    in the same way—we lie
down the hall—drowsy
    under a comforter—my
nose in the nape of
        his neck—my breast-
    bone a plane—his back-
    bone a landing lane—
my arms his arms over-
    winging—angels
        could read us at the
        same time—two writers
            writing somehow
            the same perfect line—

Barcelona, Spain

As If a Mighty Fleet

had run aground
in a harbor drained
  drained of all water
  so that only wrecks
  of ships remained
  to stand inches deep
  in sand at our feet
we hiked around them
in a drunken awe
  on a dock-like zig-zag
  trail along the draw
  their oily shadows in
  the dawn-light spilt
  across the canyon steep
until the sluggish day
had tipped it like a
dish so the sun could
noon its heat straight
down and we
  prone fish
couldn't flee too soon
that reef of leaf and
stone and spine and
pinecone and
left it alone
  to shimmer in that
  world of the mind
  only stars find.

Sedona, Arizona, USA

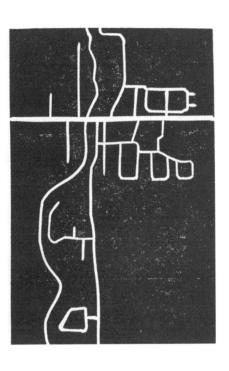

She's Going to Be Beautiful

She's going to be beautiful as she goes,
isn't she? Gorgeous plumes of cinder
blooming rose in dying light. She's going

to give a stunning show. The melting ice,
the slow decay of zones. Our drones
will play it all in full HD, and lavish insult

on the injury. All the satellite imagery.
The *National Geo* photography. She's
going to be calendar worthy stuff

if ever again a calendar there be.
Like forcing someone to disrobe
and wishing you don't want to watch.

The moon will touch her everywhere goodbye.
An elephant—the last—inelegantly,
will pass in a savannah gleaming gold.

The cloud formations no one's ever
seen, in towers shimmering with ash,
we will no longer wonder to behold.

All the coastal cities under sea. She will be
beautiful, of course she will. And
devastatingly.

Hanover, Pennsylvania, USA

Down Below the Mill Race

just around the corner from
a house I loved in France
stands a peg-and-tenon
shelter where a millwheel
once turned upon a narrow
rivulet of water that still runs
one end to the other and
from there beneath a bridge
(or rather a beam on stones
that anyone following the
stream would use as bridge)
and there's something very
peaceful about that beam so
simple the simple open-
air structure and the two
simple benches under and
the stream's sweet simplicity
its water trickling easily forth
and away and the way the
townspeople have allowed it to
stay unmarked from the street
so that one finds it accidentally
the way I imagine the insects
or the birds must find what
they find or the way streams
meander and when I lived there
for a season I loved to go there
for the simple reason that for
the time I'd spend there no
matter how long I lingered I
wouldn't have to share it with
a soul which meant such things
as lovely simple poems would
find their way to me and also

tears unbidden and sometimes
a sudden laugh at something
long thought hidden and it was
neat how an hour would turn
and the sunlight shift as if to sift
the chaff of the busy world away
from the day's sweet golden
wheat and not deplete me
but somehow fortify and
embolden me in my solitude
as if to underscore or rather
validate my more sequestered
notions which is strange to say
because it's a bit like saying
that icy springs are validated
by oceans or that time is made
of thought or that somehow time
accommodates a complicated
idea but it's true although
now that I say it out loud so
simply it doesn't seem so strange
which makes me wonder
whether poetry isn't the art of
saying strange things simply
even when saying strange things
simply means speaking rather
strangely because what is thought
after all but a kind of maze we
trace and I guess maybe mine
had lately run away from me
by the time I'd found that place
by which I mean to say that
grief or strife or life's illusions
or any number of distractions
had somehow lifted the old
mossy paddlewheel up
out of the stream to let it run

on its way without any demand
and I was grateful to have it roll
once more on dimpled water and
a little axle grease and to feel
that old pull in my mind again
and on my poem writing hand.

Tillou, Poitou-Charentes, France

An Ocean for Iowa

I don't know why. Oh, why
not, though? Don't Iowans
deserve an ocean the same
as Rhode Islanders or New
Zealanders do? We'll make it
a little one if we have to, like
the Indian. We can add it like
pork to a bill. We'll call it
the Iowan Ocean,
the Missouri will fill it, and
we won't displace anyone—
no farms will be harmed in
the pouring of this ocean—
we'll simply make a little
room in Pottawattamie or
Union County between
formerly neighboring towns
like Anita and Atlantic,
Manning and Manilla, or
Dunlap and Defiance. I'm
thinking mostly of south-
western Iowa because then
Kansans and Nebraskans
can come for the afternoon
and still get home in time
for church supper or choir,
smelling, for a change, of
salt air, their hair and clothes
blown loose by the winds
off the rich black-sand
Iowan coast. It'll mean
big changes for the economy.
Some farmers will become
lobstermen, and who could

blame them? Some, perhaps
the quieter among them,
will become seafaring men,
while others, going down
to its shores between chores,
will bring home again strings
of deliciously white-fleshed
ocean-fresh poems. And
the women, let's not forget
the women. They're going
to *adore* the ocean. It will
inspire them to do more
lovemaking, and if there's
anything Iowa needs, God
knows it's more lovemaking.
I want Iowan women, when
they're sick of looking at
corn on every horizon—
battalions of corn, frozen
in formation—to be able to
climb into the seats of
their husbands' stick-shift
Silverados and drive all 45
dirt miles of Co. Rd. H54
out of Corning past Gravity,
or east on State Hwy 30
through Glidden, Ralston,
Scranton, Jefferson,
Grand Junction, Ogden,
and Jordan, and come
at last to a dust-cloud stop
there where the cornfields
end on the bluffs overlooking
the Cape of Des Moines
or Omaha Bay, and rest
their misted soft trusting
Delft eyes awhile on the

lapped whitecapped quilt-
work of the Iowan Ocean,
then go home to their
husbands—standing in the
lamplight in their night-
cottons tumbling humble
sonnets in their heads—
and strip them like beds.
Oh, sure, there'll be some
in corner bars here or there
whose stubborn German
pride will rear at the mere
suggestion: *We don't need
no stinking ocean*, they'll
rail into their beers, *we're
Iowans, not Californians.
California's got an ocean,
what good's it done them?*
And they'll have a point:
The ocean's largely wasted
on Californians. Also New
Yorkers and Floridians. No,
an ocean's a prize uniquely
commensurate with being
Iowan: for plying the sea
of tallgrass in glass-cabined
crafts, staring deep into green;
for a lifetime's attention
to the singularly homely
flowering and fruiting of
the lowly soybean; for
shameless ministration to
the nameless and unseen—
We hereby christen this
ocean the Iowan Ocean, 8th
biggest water mass on Earth.
May it bring joy on an order

of magnitude equivalent to
the sea of corn sweetener
her refineries pour into
the food and drink factories
of the world. May it scrub
the stench from every hog
barn; dilute the pollutants,
soften every stubbornness;
un-govern every caucus;
create raucus new markets
for surf and scuba gear, for
beer and more beer chasing
lots of iced corn-whisky
shots from glasses rimmed
with salt and trimmed with
paper parasols. May every
taper dance dizzier in every
holder. May a new spirit
move upon the face of the
waters and wash across the
wheat fields, filling with a
newfound joy every sower,
crop-duster, and reaper.
And may the sky, bluer
than the blue from any
prism, fill them with a truly
nondenominational new
evangelism, truer than any
truism, and worlds deeper.

Decorah, Iowa, USA

If, as They Say, the Soul,

in the vast abyss before time,
does indeed commingle first
with light and earth and mist
and then with self, and then
at last with something more
than self, an energy, before
becoming stone and sinking
back into the bliss of light
or antilight or the light of life
we call the afterlife, releasing
self to burn like spun debris,
then this—this *now*—or God,
 if we allow there is a God, or
something metaphysical in me
or you—must alchemize the
transubstantiation in the coal,

and since this *now* is not so
new, when taken, eons, all at
once, and since my solitary
soul is none supreme, and since
God's will must be forever
strange, just as our dreams
make strange what's true, it
seems to me it's you, my dear
and rare and lustrous friend—
star about which my stars bend—
who does the blessed alchemy,
or, if not you, perhaps it's us—
the chance transversity of us—

our difference and its valency—
power amplified in twinning—
that keeps the cosmic deeps
inside me spinning.

after Ursula K. Le Guin, "How It Seems to Me"
Brisbane, Australia

Tracers

Let's say one day
the ballgame from
the day before mys-
teriously rematerial-
izes in the form of
tracers—each pitch,
each hit, each catch,
each toss, each
criss and crisscross
marked—chalked
in air—here, there—
reiterated, the way a
window, fogged,
remembers the last
things third graders
wrote with fingers
on it. Let's say it
rendered the field
unplayable so they
let you walk it.
They would. It'd be
a big attraction—
tracers interlacing,
crepe paper streamers
of a pastime past,
most between bases
and the rest of the
bands connecting
home plate with
the outfield or even
the stands in some
cases—inning on
inning of contrails
twinning and twining

in defining strands
as if the ball'd been
string. It might
not mean anything
but it would be odd.
My god, you'd say
at the sight, ducking
the not-quite-straight
line of a line drive to
right, remarking how
much of the game,
which seemed so
grounded last night,
is in fact in flight—
pure energy trans-
ferred from giving
hand to waiting
glove, the way our
lives are made of
thought and love
and word and prayer
in particle or wave
surrounding every
numbered and un-
numbered player
on the planet in a
dome of light
that stadiums us,
immense, between
the dugout caves we
crawled from and
that elusive
outfield fence.

Risk Not One

Complicate your life. Confuse it.
What good's a plot if you don't use it?
The Wire, S1, Episode 10—
nothing was at stake till then,
so the story didn't matter much.
The game got real. Until you clutch
your bedsheets to your chin, life's just
TV, a show. No—nonplussed
is how you want to go. Confounded.
Trees and shrubs and grubs are grounded,
we rate Biblical complications:
tainted loves, corrupted nations,
angry gods. Play the odds. Go for broke.
Quit your comforts. Face the smoke.
Use your fears to file your knives.
Risk not one but all your lives.

Page, Arizona, USA

Always That Last Trip to the Airport

in a taxi . . . always the city through
the windows seeming unexplored,
no matter how exhaustively I toured.
Always the temptation to cancel
flights and remain, a new resident.
If the world is, aren't I too in pencil,
a sketch of a man? It's no accident
I'm grafted here, drafted here, a
figure stenciled on a foreign scene,
rogue, but increasingly road weary,
denizen of the requisite in-between.
Not all who march march for a cause.
I travel like some drink—to be lost.
My bags may as well be stuffed with
gauze for all the blood my journey's
cost. Then: *Airline?* asks the driver.
I check my phone. I can't remember.
We seem to be here early. We seem
to have navigated the stars. Seems
I've been studying my chauffeur in
the mirror—tanned *Britannica*, brown-
eyed Qur'an—reading and re-reading
there, I swear: How I could love. How
I could love anyone. How I could love
anyone and anywhere.

Marrakesh, Morocco

In the Verbena, the Bees

are auxiliary verbs again:

am

is

are

was

were

be

being

been . . .

ACKNOWLEDGMENTS AND NOTES

I'm grateful to the periodicals in which these poems from *Someday the Plan of a Town* first appeared, sometimes in slightly edited versions:

32 Poems	"Everything I Have Has Humps and Hooves"
	"The Mind Will Wander"
Left Hooks	"The Sculptor Made a Giant of the Boy"
Minnesota Public Radio's *All Things Considered*	
	"An Ocean for Iowa"
New Ohio Review	"Tracers"
	"Essentials"
	"He Divides His Time Between"
South Carolina Review	"Golds Within"
Terrain.org	"She's Going to Be Beautiful"

"The Mind Will Wander" was anthologized in *What Light*, a publication of MNartists.org.

   "Risk Not One" was adapted for solo voice by composer Matt Boehler and premiered and recorded by mezzo-soprano Sasha Cooke.

"She's Going to Be Beautiful" was nominated for a Pushcart Prize by Terrain.org; special thanks to editors Simmons Buntin and Derek Sheffield. It was included in *Dear America: Letters of Hope, Habitat, Defiance, and Democracy* (Simmons Buntin, Elizabeth Dodd, and Derek Sheffield, eds.), Trinity University Press, 2020.

The following poems are dedicated to the following people: "As If a Mighty Fleet" is for Hila Plitmann. "Be Glad Your Parents Fucked" is for my parents. "If, as They Say, the Soul" was commissioned by Constance Holmes to honor her long friendship with Jean Kilbourne. "I Know You Feel You're the Wyeth Girl and that the Farmhouse Yonder" is for Mallory Capri Henson. "Someday the Plan of a Town" is for Spencer Reece and Joanne Harris. "Tracers" is for Kay Ryan. "When the Sommelier Farts" was commissioned by Chris Causey to honor the fiftieth birthday of Paul Mahon, and was written during a residency at Write On, Door County, thanks to Jerod Santek.

Special thanks to the following individuals who support my work on Patreon.com: Amanda Thornell, Constance L. Holmes, Dawn Bradley, Deb Brooks, Elaine Wang Meyerhoffer, Elizabeth E. Wilder, Ethna McKiernan, Hervey Evans, Jeanie Tomasko, Jenny Hermanson, Jack Miles, Julie Stroud, Lisa Angelella, Lori Crever, Mallory Henson, Marisha Chamberlain, Marsha O'Neil, Rachel Greene, Rachel Williams, Vikki Glodek, Hila Plitmann.

For all their hard work on my behalf, I am grateful to my editor, Jill Bialosky, and my assistant, Mallory Capri Henson.

For their superabundance of energy in support of this book and other recent projects, I'm grateful to Jack and Cheri Boss, Jake Runestad, Vaughn Ormseth, Matt Boehler, Harrison Rivers, Irve Dell, Ilya Kaminsky, Graywolf Press, Jorell Williams, Daniel Slager, Matt Piermantier, Andrew Gamson, Andy Reynolds, Jennifer Dodgson, Pacyinz Lyfoung, Aaron Bauer, Glenis Redmond, Sarah Wolfe, Ryan Stopera, Julie Stroud, Maija Hecht, Cara Storm, Ray Berry, Roxanne Artesona, Jon Hallberg, Cera Crockett, Rock Galpin, Indie Do Good, Jack Becker, Pixel Farm Creative, Susannah Schouweiler, Tricia Heuring, Nicole J. Caruth, Matthew Fluharty, Marlena Myles, Sam Van Aken, Sheryl Winarick, Jim Moore, Kirsten Dierking, Tim Nolan, Tracy Youngblom, Dore Kiesselbach, Sharon Chmielarz, Liz Weir, Rubin Pfeffer, Ronan Mattin's family, the Handel and Haydn Society, Adam Smith, Joan Vorderbruggen.

ABOUT THE AUTHOR

©2019 Mallory Capri Henson

Todd Boss is a poet, public artist, inventor, librettist, and film producer. His large-scale public artworks include a building projection, multimedia installations, and virtual reality/augmented reality projects. His lyrics have been performed at the Kennedy Center, Carnegie Hall, and around the world. He is the founding artistic director of Motionpoems, a production company that has turned more than 150 contemporary poems into short films. He is the inventor of the Laptop Strap family of business accessories, and of the American Unity Flag. *Someday the Plan of a Town* is his fourth collection from W. W. Norton & Co. More at toddbossoriginals.com.

ABOUT THE ARTIST

Aislynn Palmer

Pamela Gerbrandt is a former art educator, now parent and artist. She grew up in a small town and has always been drawn to maps and the significance that places can have in our memories and experiences. Celebrating small towns with small, simple linocut prints seemed like a perfect way to acknowledge these often overlooked places. Find more of her work in her Etsy shop, NiceArtPeople.